Beads AT PLAY Genius ON THE WAY

"How abacus education helps unleash your child's true potential."

Beads AT PLAY Genius ON THE WAY

"How abacus education helps unleash your child's true potential."

Dr. GAURAV MITTAL

Published Internationally by
Pendown Press
Powered by Gullybaba.com

PENDOWN PRESS
Powered by **Gullybaba Publishing House Pvt. Ltd.,**
An ISO 9001 & ISO 14001 Certified Co.,
Regd. Office: 2525/193, 1st Floor, Onkar Nagar-A, Tri Nagar, Delhi-110035
Ph.: 09350849407, 09312235086
E-mail: info@pendownpress.com
Branch Office: 1A/2A, 20, Hari Sadan, Ansari Road, Daryaganj, New Delhi-110002
Ph.: 011-45794768
Website: PendownPress.com

First Edition: 2021
Price: ₹299/-
ISBN: 978-93-90479-88-7

Layout Design: Pendown Press Publishing
Printed and bound in India by Thomson Press India Ltd.

DEDICATION

This book is dedicated to my family who has always supported me, worked together, and participated as a team.

This book is also dedicated to all my associates working in the field of Abacus Education, whom I have ever met or come across in the last 15 years of my association with this industry.

References

The book has taken content references from various websites on the Internet. This book has a few illustrations designed using resources from freepik.com

CONTENTS

PREFACE

In the last 20 years, abacus education centres have mushroomed all over India. Numerous abacus and mental arithmetic centres have opened in every nook and corner of big cities and small towns alike. They run in setups as small as a dining table of a 1 BHK flat to as big as a 10-room commercial space with play area and greens.

If one takes a wild guess, there may be around 25,000+ abacus centres running in India today. The best performing ones may have about 300 or more children in them and the not-so-well performing ones may have as few as 3-5 children. The average strength would be around 50-60 children per centre. This means around 1.2 million students are currently enrolled in these abacus institutes and approximately another 2 million may have enrolled and completed their program in the past 20 years. Statistically speaking, these are good numbers for an educational program that is not mandatory as per the Indian education system.

The abacus institutions generally run in the franchisee model barring a few who wander around independently. The franchisee model has its own advantages, provided the centre is attached to a good franchisor.

Success stories of good abacus franchisors trigger herd instincts in others, resulting in the evolution of incongruous players, who do not have much insight into the abacus program. These incongruous players cause quality problems.

Broadly, abacus education has been unorganized due to the absence of any regulation from the government. The practices followed by big players have become the de facto industry standard.

Most parents enrol their child in an abacus program, probably because one of their neighbours or relatives suggested to do so or parents of their child's friend have referred them or spoken highly about it. Most of the people, who recommend the abacus program, themselves, are not much aware about it but have been awestruck by the performance of their child.

On the flip side, those parents who fell victim to inappropriate centres lose trust in the concept. A few myths and doubts about the concept too float around, which prevent prospective parents from concluding whether to get their child registered for an abacus program or not. If they decide to go ahead, a few questions arises like; How do they select the right centre? Are there any ill effects?

In general, if you ask parents about what an abacus program is, lots of times, the answer is greeted with a blank face. Abacus programs have always been treated as a mathematics program by most parents. In the numerous awareness sessions that I have done with parents, I generally began with a question; "What do you know about the abacus program?" The preponderance of responses has been around the abacus being a mathematics program or a program that helps improve the children's mathematical skills.

Arithmetic has been the basis or foundation of the abacus program, but it is not solely a mathematics program. It is also about brain and cognitive skill development.

This limited awareness has motivated me to write this book. I have spent a good 15 years in the field of abacus education and have seen the best, the good, the bad and the ugly of abacus education very closely.

This book will help:

- Parents who have been unaware of how the abacus program work. They will know about it and understand how it will benefit their children.
- Parents who have enrolled their kids or plan to enrol them. It will help them take considerate decisions regarding; Why their child should enrol in the abacus program? Where should they join? What is the right age? Why there is an age criterion? What is the right methodology? What are the best practices? This book will set the expectations right. They will also understand the difference between abacus and other maths programs available, especially the vedic maths.
- Prospective abacus education franchisees or centre owners to take the right decisions on how and why to start an abacus centre.
- Existing franchisees to rightly counsel parents.

- Educators or course instructors to understand the importance of right training and deliver more diligently.

I hope that this book will help you take the right decision as a parent or as an enterprising individual. That way, I will be able to achieve my objective.

Happy reading!!

CHAPTER 1

INTRODUCTION

"Make your child faster than a calculator"
"Beads at play, genius on the way"
"Whole Brain Development"
"Make your child genius they were born to become"
"Discover the genius in your child"

Most of us have seen these taglines in numerous advertisements across media platforms by various Abacus education centres and have always wondered if this is possible? How can a child possibly calculate faster than a calculator?

Most likely, you would have seen a few demonstration videos circulating on YouTube/WhatsApp/Facebook or had an opportunity to witness a live demonstration session by young children, where they are moving their fingers in the air and solving large arithmetic questions with great speed and high accuracy.

These demonstrations would have surely awed you, and you wished your children could do these calculations, with the same speed and accuracy. Afterall, mathematics has been the biggest phobia for most students, and the demo that you have just seen seems to be the best remedy.

For those who have not seen any of the above, let us assume an arithmetic question, where the child is expected to add the following numbers:

784 + 622 + 230 + 632 + 775 + 426 + 587 + 298 + 944 + 305 + 440 + 448

Usually, a child would require a pen and a paper and about 60 to 75 seconds to answer 6491. But a student who has done the abacus program from a good centre will be able to solve it mentally, without pen and paper, and that too in just about 3-5 seconds. This is affirmatively quicker than the time one would take to solve it using the calculator.

To a spectator, such a performance will make him believe that the child has excellent mathematical skills. For a child to answer this question in such a short time without pen and paper would require few more skills in addition to the mathematical skills like concentration, memory, accuracy, processing speed, listening skills, comprehension, etc.

These abilities are called cognitive skills and are associated with the human brain. Enhancing these skills will improve a child's performance in almost every sphere of life. Each of these cognitive skills play an important part in the learning process. A weak cognitive skill has an adverse effect on learning abilities like grasping, retaining, or utilizing information by a child. In fact, all children who struggle with learning will have one or more frail cognitive skills.

For interested and prudent parents, this performance display is overwhelming and a lot of questions arise in their mind: *What is abacus? How does it work? How does the abacus, a counting device, help improve cognitive skills? Will my child get confused, as he or she has been doing arithmetic questions using the school method?* And many more…

The abacus is a counting device with a frame made from wood or plastic. Within the frame, there are vertical rods carrying beads. These rods signify the place value in the place value system. Each of these beads mounted on a vertical rod have a specific value. These beads help the child visualize numbers in the form of an image.

Abacus is useful in carrying out arithmetical operations like counting, addition, subtraction, multiplication, division, exponents, roots, etc.

However, when coupled with the knowledge of functionality and working of human brain, the abacus can help improve the cognitive abilities in a child.

We can define an abacus program as an educational program that uses the abacus as a tool and arithmetic as a medium to enhance the cognitive skills of the children in the age group of 5+ to 13 years.

It gives an edge and a strong advantage to the children in this competitive world. More and more children are joining the abacus program and availing the benefit it imparts, polishing their cognitive skills. These children then set remarkably high-performance benchmarks that become the new normal. The children who opt out fail to get the bounty of benefits.

Let us play a quiz about your child

1. My child makes careless mistakes in schoolwork or during other activities. Yes/No.
2. My child regularly/quite often losses things at school like books and stationery. Yes/No.
3. My child has problem concentrating while studying, doing tasks or playing. Yes/No.
4. My child regularly/quite often forgets things, chores, activities, etc. Yes/No.
5. My child does not seem to listen seriously when spoken to directly. Yes/No.
6. My child loses focus very soon and gets easily distracted when a task is started. Yes/No.
7. My child has problems with time management and organizing tasks. Yes/No.
8. My child has problems doing sustained activities like writing full length examination papers or long activities. Yes/No.

If you have answered seven or more questions as "No," all seem to be right for your child, and the only way should be upwards when it comes to progress if the status is maintained. The abacus program will act as a catalyst in the journey.

If your answers have been otherwise, the child seems to have serious attention deficit issues. The attention deficit could be due to multiple reasons but one of the biggest known culprits has been the use of technology.

These days, children have easy access to mobiles, tablets, PCs, and laptops, which result in high screen timing. Some mobile brands have started capturing the total screen time in a day that gives you clear information about how much screen time is reasonable and how much time is being spent looking into the phone. High screen time negatively affects the child's cognitive skills like concentration or attention spans.

With every passing year, the human attention spans have been reducing. The average attention span or time humans could concentrate in the year 2000 was about 12 seconds. While we are in 2021, this time has reduced to 7 seconds. Visualize the impact this has on our children.

Recommending a divorce with technology cannot be a practical solution. The use of technology will continue to increase exponentially as the digital screen expands beyond mobiles and tablets into almost all the devices surrounding us. Internet of Things is the next big bet by most technology behemoths. This means that the digital footprint will only increase. The cognitive abilities of our children will continue to be the victim.

The abacus program is the remedy which could help reverse the negative effect of technology and enable your child to overcome the growing attention span deficit.

Enrolling your child in an abacus program could help unleash your child's true potential and craft the genius he or she is born to become.

CHAPTER 2

COGNITIVE SKILLS

A typical class in a regular school has about 30-40 children. All of them get similar guidance, the same infrastructure, an identical set of instructions, and nearly equal opportunities. Yet, no two children perform in the same way, be it in academics, sports, or co-curricular activities.

Assume a family consisting of parents and two children. Both these children enjoy nearly similar upbringing and parenting, yet the two perform differently.

Even in the case of twins, having almost identical situations in school and home, their performance and personalities vary.

The question that arises is, "What are the differentiating factors that bring around variances in the performance of two children?"

The differentiating factors that affect every child's performance are the various cognitive skills they possess.

A few children may have some imbibed talents, in certain cases, but then they are exceptional.

Talent and skills are two different things. Talent is a unique, natural and inborn ability of a person to do something in a way that attracts appreciation and admiration. Talent is God gifted. A skill is an expertise acquired by the person by continuous learning. Skill is an ability you develop after putting in your time and sustained effort.

Cognitive skills are the core skills that a human brain uses to think, imagine, read, write, memorize, remember, reason, comprehend, observe, concentrate, etc. Almost everything we do utilizes one or the other of these cognitive skills. These can also be referred to as brain skills.

As we go further, we will understand various cognitive skills and realize that every aspect of life is related and governed by them.

Concentration is one of the cognitive skills. At one point or the other, most parents complained that their child lacks concentration skills. They fret that their child is restless or does not pay attention to essential things.

So, what is concentration? How can we measure concentration? How can we improve it? How does abacus help us to improve concentration? How can we assess objectively if the concentration has improved? We will be able to answer these questions as we progress.

All children have cognitive skills, more or less. But like all other skills, these skills too can be developed, enhanced and mastered.

Abacus program is a prominent and efficient one to achieve this objective. The abacus program is also referred as the "Whole brain development program" or "Abacus and mental arithmetic program".

Let us understand some of these cognitive skills in detail to understand the significance and how they help us in day-to-day life. How on enhancement, these skills increase a person's learning abilities and overall personality exponentially?

Some of the cognitive skills are listed below with detailed analysis. As we discuss these, we will try to derive analogy with real life examples for better understanding:

1. **Listening Skills:** It is the ability to remember and understand auditory information. The information that one has just heard to for a limited span of time. Information like, "remembering the name of somebody you just met", "telephone number or address that was given", "listen to a radio contest, then remember the multiple-choice answers provided and then listen to a telephone number where the answer has to be sent".

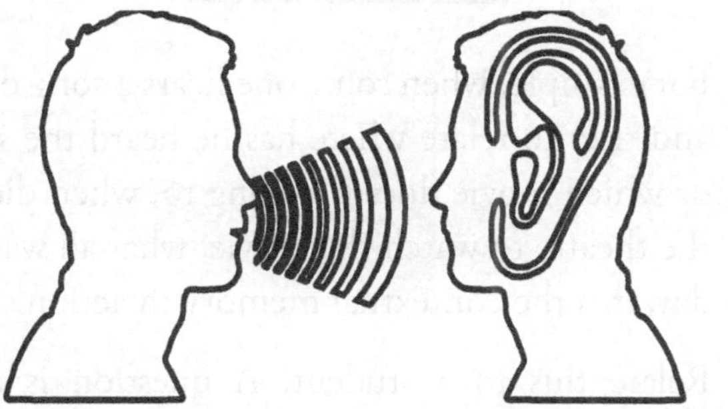

For students, remembering the teacher's lecture and simultaneously taking notes with ease is important.

Many mistakes occur in the little time gap, between teacher delivering a lecture and students taking notes. The children with weak listening skills need more time to recognize and process the information they have heard. This makes it difficult for them to understand and make them frustrated and feel incompetent. These children will then need to re-read the content again or take additional classes to keep up.

2. **Contextual Memory:** Contextual memory is the brain's ability to recall information, along with the conscious recall of the source and circumstances of this specific memory.

For example, when some one hears a song on the radio and tries to relate where has he heard the song before or which movie does it belong to, when did they visit the theatre to watch the movie, what all was done that day, it is the contextual memory in action.

Relate this to a student. A question is asked, and the child not only recalls the answer, but also all the relevant information that were provided by the teacher during the session when the topic was discussed. The child will be in a better position to thoroughly answer the question with examples.

3. **Multitasking:** The ability to execute more than one action or attending to two or more stimuli at the same time. This cognitive skill enhances the efficiency of a person.

While driving on road, a driver multi tasks by looking at the road, reading the road signs, listening to radio, controlling the car, all at the same time. Imagine if the driver is not able to do multitasking, do you think driving will be possible?

Multitasking is an essential factor for a student. Being able to understand what the teacher is saying while reading the board and taking notes simultaneously are tasks that are essential to successful learning.

4. **Concentration or Attention:** The ability to focus on a single task over a period of time despite distractions or having multiple tasks to perform at once.

Taking the previous example of multitasking, the driver carries out multiple tasks, but his or her focus is purely on driving on the road, on the route, traffic, and road signs. Factors like listening to the radio, talking on the phone, reading billboards, etc., should not divert his or her attention.

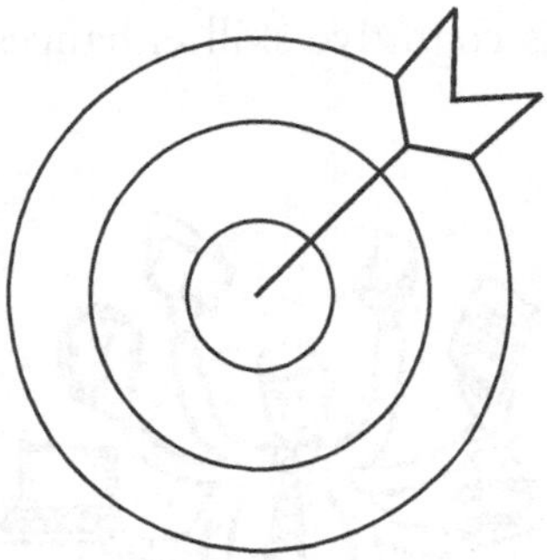

If a student pays attention to what the teacher is explaining in the class, the learning and understanding will be much better, compared to those who keep looking out from the window or scribbling on their notebooks.

A person's concentration can be easily affected by multiple factors—internal factors like feeling thirsty, sleepy, happy or sad and external factors like the ringing of telephone or doorbell, etc.

5. **Comprehension:** It is the ability to understand a new concept.

   While studying a language, reading comprehension is a regular exercise where the student reads a paragraph and based on the understanding of the paragraph, certain questions need to be answered. In the real-life scenario, this cognitive skill helps us understand the new theories, concepts, and technology.

Decades ago, computers were a fantasy. Back then, they weren't widely adopted. As time passed, many people started adopting and comprehending the working of computers. Although many had no formal training on the computer, this adoption was happening. The earliest computers didn't come with slick manuals and tech support; much progress came from hobbyists who figured out things for themselves! Similarities can be drawn for smartphones also. However, if the comprehension skills are not strong, we will find it difficult to adopt these technological advancements.

The most sought-after professions of the future may not even exist today and are not part of the formal education structure. It is this cognitive skill of comprehension that helps us in learning today as well as preparing us for the future as well.

6. **Eye Hand Coordination:** This is the ability to do activities that require the simultaneous use of hands and eyes. This is one of the most complex cognitive skills.

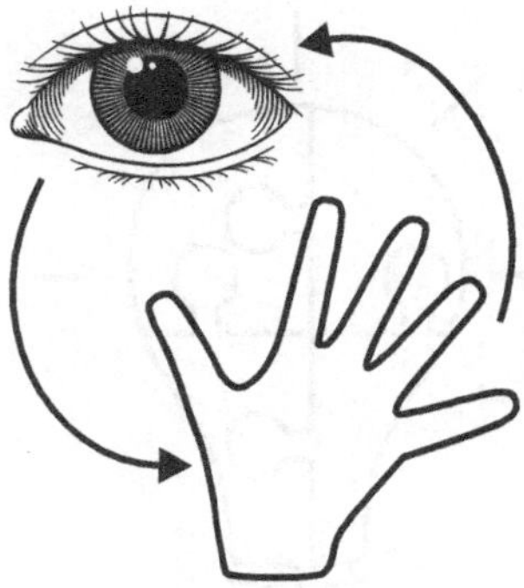

The eye sends the information to the brain, which processes it, and then sends instruction to the hands or legs to execute.

Eye-hand coordination is the primary skill that we use to write. As one starts making lines, the eyes send visual information to the brain to tell it where the hand is placed and if the handwriting is legible. With this information, the brain generates instructions for how the hand must move to create appropriate lines and shapes, resulting in letters.

While driving, the driver continually uses eye-hand coordination by using the visual information to move hands on the wheel or brakes, in order to safely drive the car.

7. **Inhibition:** The ability to ignore irrelevant reactions while performing a task is the Inhibition cognitive skill.

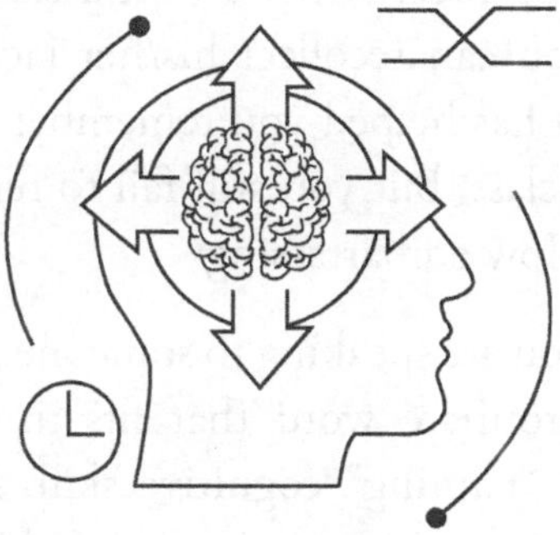

The urge to look at the phone every now and then, walking to the kitchen repeatedly to get something to eat while studying, gossiping in between important tasks, etc., are often distractions to completing the important work we really want to get done. A successful student will inhibit these actions and likely perform better academically.

8. **Naming:** The ability to recall a word from our logical vocabulary is also a cognitive skill. It is a basic ability that helps you while speaking.

W	Z	J	Q	R	A	E	L	C
D	I	L	A	X	F	O	H	Z
G	U	K	P	I	N	Z	M	X
U	A	B	A	C	U	S	Z	D
N	E	V	H	Q	K	A	M	G
L	W	A	F	P	J	R	U	B
A	C	O	G	N	I	T	O	R
D	X	Q	S	U	R	L	P	N
G	H	J	M	E	W	B	A	F

When you meet a friend (like a classmate) after many years, you can recollect his/her face, your contextual memory has helped you remember that he or she was in your class, but you still fail to remember his or her name. How embarrassing!

When you are speaking to someone and fail to recollect the appropriate word that fits in the sentence, you lack the "naming" cognitive skill. Imagine a student appearing for an examination, which has a question "Where is the Taj Mahal?" The student could recollect how Taj Mahal looks using contextual memory but would need the naming cognitive skill to recall Agra as the correct answer.

9. **Planning or Judgement:** The ability to "think ahead" or anticipate the path or flow of a task. What will happen if I do this? The ability to foresee outcomes of certain steps, while solving a problem is "Judgement" cognitive skill.

Packing your bag for a trip, preparing a To-Do list or shopping list are certain planning skills that we exhibit albeit at different efficiency levels. People who are poor at planning skills, are unable to take decisions, calculate or estimate proper timelines to complete their actions; they get easily distracted and become forgetful.

10. **Processing Speed:** Processing speed is one of the most important cognitive processes, which relates to fluency, or how fast we can think or process information. It is the time taken by an individual to understand and react to the information received. It is a critical skill for learning, academic performance, intellectual development, reasoning, and experience. Processing speed implies a greater ability to do simple or previously learned tasks easily.

Sometimes, a child with slow processing speed takes a while to answer a simple question like 3 + 4. If a child can finish an assignment in 15 minutes, which is done by other children in 30 minutes, it will surely be a big boost to his or her performance.

11. **Recognition:** The ability to retrieve information from the past and to recognize certain events, places, or other information. Recognition is a cognitive ability that

makes it possible to recover stored data and compare it to the information being presented in front of you.

During an exam, it is crucial that a student correctly recognizes what a certain question is referring to. If the student is unable to recognize the chapter or information related to the particular question, it may lead the student to failure in exam. When you are driving, you must be able to recognize what road you should take in order to reach your destination, you must be aware of the route so that you can take the right turns.

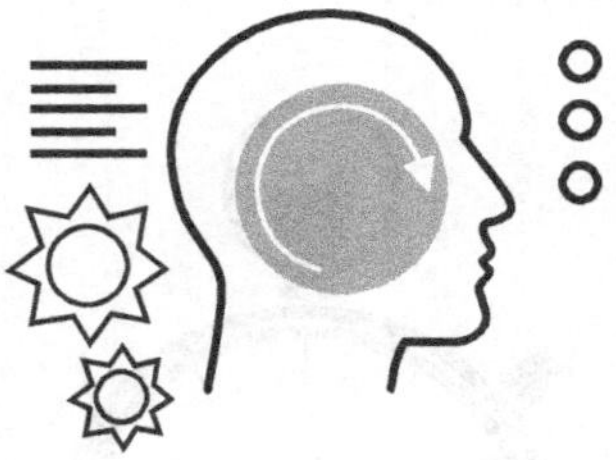

12. **Response Time:** The ability to perceive and process a simple stimulus and respond to it. Reaction time or response time refers to the amount of time taken to perceive something and respond to it accordingly.

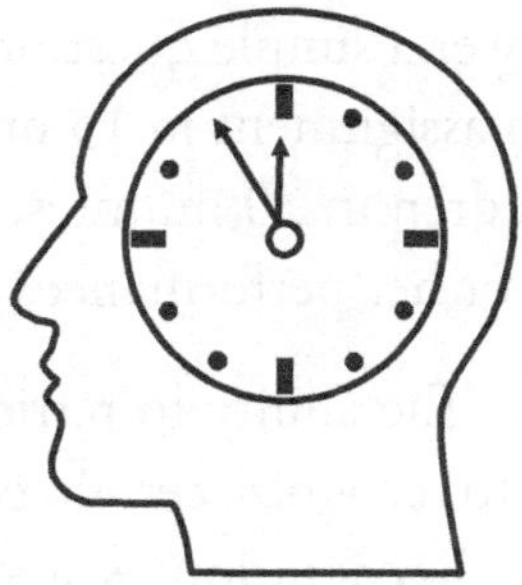

Reaction time depends on various factors:

- **Perception:** Seeing, hearing, or feeling a stimulus with certainty is essential to have a good reaction time. Let us take an example of a race, where the athletes will start when they hear the whistle. The athlete's ears receive the whistle's sound (they perceive the stimulus).
- **Processing:** In order to have a good reaction time, it is necessary to be focused and understand the information well. Following the previous example, after hearing the whistle, the runners will be able to distinguish the sound from other background noise and know that it is time to start running (process the stimulus).
- **Response:** Motor agility is necessary to act and have a good response time. When the runners perceive and correctly process the signal, they start moving their legs (respond to the stimulus).

Red light → Need to stop → Apply break

(Perceive) (Process) (Response)

Smoke → Danger → Get fire extinguisher

(Perceive) (Process) (Response)

13. **Flexibility or Shifting:** Shifting is the ability to see that what you are doing is not working and make the appropriate changes to adapt to new situations.

You always take the same route to work. One day, it is raining, and you know that there will be traffic jams. What do you do? Change the route or may be leave early. The cognitive flexibility or shifting allows to think of possible alternative solutions to help get work done efficiently.

14. **Spatial Perception:** The ability to evaluate how things are arranged in space and investigate their relations in the environment.

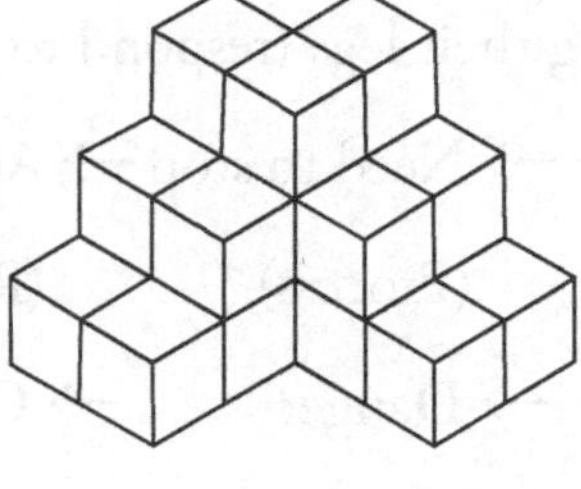

Good spatial awareness allows us to understand the environment and our relationship to it. Spatial perception also consists of understanding the relationship between two objects when there is a change in their position in space. It helps us think in two and three dimensions, which allows us to visualize objects from different angles and recognize them, no matter the perspective that we see them from.

Spatial perception is important and useful for people of all ages, as we are constantly using this cognitive ability. For example, when we walk, dress ourselves, or even draw. Poor spatial perception affects how we focus. Another example would be that our spatial perception continually prevents us from walking into walls, chairs, doors, etc. While driving, the driver uses spatial perception to judge if it is safe to overtake. In these cases, we must judge the distance, position, and dimension of other objects in relation to ourselves.

15. **Non-Verbal Memory:** The ability to store and retrieve information which is non-verbal by nature. Non-verbal memory is the ability to code, store, and recover information about faces, shapes, images, songs, sounds, smells, tastes, and feelings. Non-verbal memory makes it possible to retain and remember content without words (neither written nor spoken). This is an important skill and is used in several daily activities.

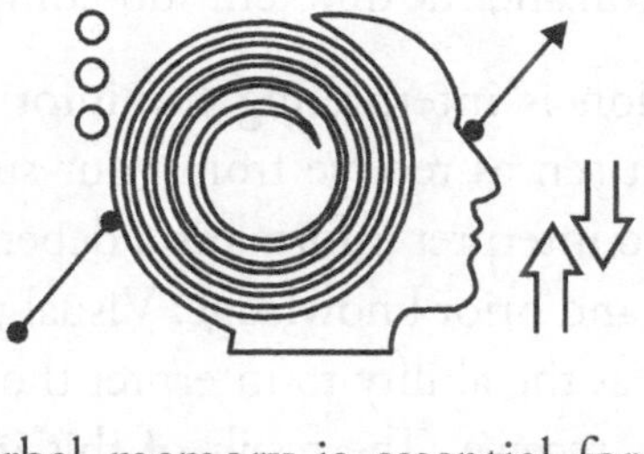

Non-verbal memory is essential for a wide range of careers, like architecture, designers, musicians or other artists, etc.

Students use non-verbal memory daily, whether it is to remember a map, draw a picture, or create a technical outline. Young children also have different textures in their classrooms to help them learn through touch.

You use non-verbal memory when remembering how to go to a new restaurant or friend's house.

16. **Perception:** The ability to interpret information from the effects of visible light reaching the eye.

Being able to read this text seems like a simple process. We look at the letters and make sense of the words. It seems simple, but it is an extremely complex process that uses several brain structures specialized in visual perception and the different sub-components of vision.

Perception is interpreting the information that your different senses receive from your surroundings. This ability to interpret information depends on a cognitive process and prior knowledge. Visual perception can be defined as the ability to interpret the information that our eyes receive. The result of this information being interpreted and received by the brain is what we call visual perception, vision or sight.

Driving is one of the most complex daily tasks that many people do every day. It requires many different complex processes, one of which is visual perception. If one of the processes in visual perception fails, it may endanger the driver and the people around. It is so important to figure out quickly how close two cars are to each other, how fast they are going, etc., which would not be possible if your visual perception is poor.

A child in the class will benefit greatly from developed visual perception, as it will allow the child to take notes and better understand the reading material in general. An alteration or deficiency in this skill may result in poor academic performance.

In the visual arts, like painting or graphic design, visual perception is significant. If you want to draw a square that really is a square, and not a rhombus, or a circle that is even, you need visual perception to measure and draft your lines well.

17. **Visual Scanning or Observation:** It is the ability to actively find relevant information in our surroundings quickly and efficiently.

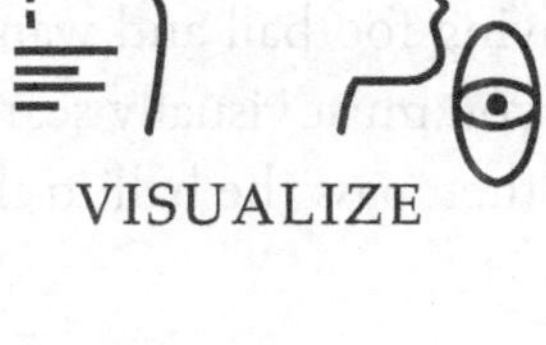

VISUALIZE

Visual scanning is the ability to efficiently, quickly, and actively look for information relevant to your environment. It makes you find what you are looking for by using your vision. Visual scanning is an important skill for daily life as it helps to carry out different tasks efficiently.

Police officers or members of the military must be able to quickly and precisely detect objects that may be dangerous. Store employees must use visual scanning to keep an eye out for products that may be out of place. Almost every job has some visual component level that requires good visual scanning.

Students are constantly using visual scanning at school, whether it is to pay attention to the board, read a book or understand a presentation. It would be difficult to study new material if the students are unable to find the word or idea in their notes or textbooks when they are trying to review the information before a test.

Driving requires constant lookout for other cars, perception of accidents, potential hazards, traffic signs, pedestrians and several other objects or situations.

Visual scanning is an essential part of playing sports. Most sports require quick and precise scanning of the space for stimuli, which may be teammates, rivals, a ball, goal or any other vital component of the game. If you are playing football and want to pass the ball to a teammate, you must visually scan the field to find him or her and then pass the ball to the intended person.

There are many more cognitive skills like imagination, creativity, application, reasoning, self-confidence, self-analysis, etc. Some of these are self-explanatory, some less so.

Understanding the significance and relevance of cognitive skills in a student's life is of prime importance. The prime purpose of an abacus program is to improve all these cognitive skills. These skills not just find importance in academics, but sports, music, art, dance, writing, driving, cooking, talking, etc. In fact, they are the backbone of everything that we do.

CHAPTER 3

THE HUMAN BRAIN

Since we have now understood cognitive skills, the next logical step in our quest is understanding our brain. After all, cognitive skills arise from the brain. Once we get basic insight into this complex organ and how we can reach it, we can explore ways to mould it.

The human brain is an intricate organ. It is a labyrinthine structure consisting of billions of neurons making trillions of connections. It is the body's central command system. The human brain is always in learning mode through experience. It is tailor-made to learn and is always changing.

We will analyse the brain's function from three perspectives:

- **Logical**
- **Biological**
- **Chronological**

Logical Functioning

Logically, the brain is divided into two halves or hemispheres. Multiple theories have given it various names or classifications like left and right, logical and artistic, verbal and non-verbal brain, etc. Each of these halves controls certain functions in our body. The two sides of our brain look similar, but the way the information is processed by the two are different. If we look at the brain, it looks like a symmetric organ, just like the entire human body. But functionally, it is asymmetric. The two sides have their own functionality.

The left hemisphere is verbal and analytical in functionality. It is sometimes called the logical brain and is generally referred to as temporary or short-term in nature. It is better at things like reading, writing, and computations.

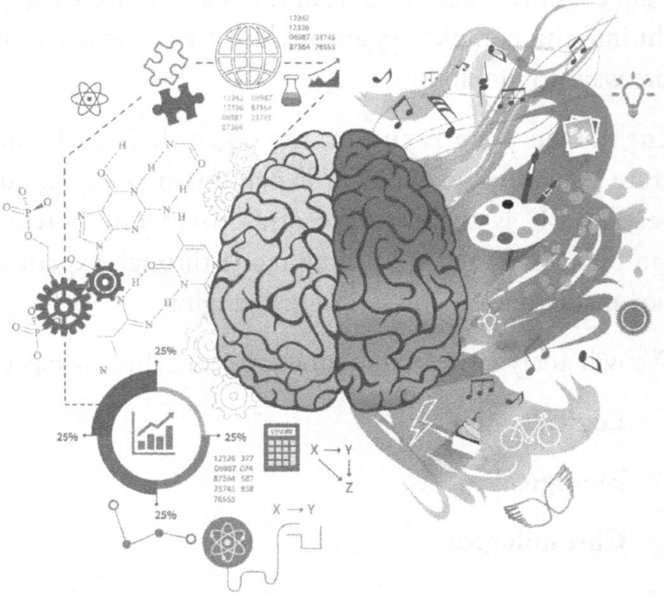

The left brain is associated with logic, sequencing, linear thinking, mathematics, facts, thinking in words, etc.

The right brain is more visual and intuitive. It is sometimes referred to as the artistic brain and is considered permanent or long-term. It has a more creative and less organized way of thinking. The right brain is associated with imagination, holistic thinking, intuition, arts, rhythm, non-verbal cues, feelings, visualization, daydreaming, etc.

Parents have always advised their children to write to memorize the course content. All of us have heard a quite common statement- "*Likh likh kar yaad karo*" (memorize by writing again and again). The logic is that when you write, you form an image of the text which is processed in the right side of the brain, and when you try to memorize by reading or repeating orally, the information is processed in the left side of the brain. The left side is temporary, and children tend to forget sooner when they read vis a vis when they write, the right side of the brain being permanent, they tend to remember for a longer duration.

Suppose we meet a friend or even an acquaintance after years, our normal thought is "I have seen him before, but I cannot remember the name". Face (picture) was processed in our right brain and has been retained for longer times, whereas name was processed in our left brain and could not be easily recalled.

This theory of the brain's two hemispheres functioning differently came to light in the 1960s, thanks to Nobel Prize winner Roger W. Sperry's research. But with time, as more and more research is being conducted, alternate and scientifically supported theories are emerging.

The two sides of our brain are different, but does it necessarily follow or mean that we have a dominant brain just as we have a dominant hand? No. The two halves have their distinctive roles, but they work concurrently.

MRIs (Magnetic Resonance Imaging) of people revealed that human brain does not take sides. The two hemispheres are tied together by bundles of nerve fibres, creating an information highway. Although the two sides function differently, they work together and complement each other. You do not use only one side of your brain at a time.

Whether you are performing a logical or creative function, you receive input from both sides of your brain. For example, the left brain processes the language, but the right brain will help you understand the context of the same. The left brain handles mathematical equations, but the right brain helps in comparisons and rough estimates.

General personality traits, individual preferences, or learning style do not translate into the idea that you are left-brained or right-brained.

Generally, people are either right-handed or left-handed. Another research using MRI scans revealed that motor cortex (the part of the brain that controls the motor skills or body movement, like walking), is bigger on the left side for right-handers and bigger on right side for left-handers.

The left hemisphere controls the muscles on the right side of the body, while the right hemisphere controls those on the left.

Therefore, using the hand or foot or muscles of the left side of the body will be like exercising to the right side of the brain and using the right side of the body will be similar to exercising the left side of the brain.

Our day-to-day functioning focuses on one side of muscle being exercised.

The method followed by the students while using the abacus requires using both the hands in symmetry with each other so that both sides of the brain exercise together.

Important concern on forcing left handers to become right handers:

Before we progress to the next brain functioning classification we will digress for an important issue. There are numerous instances where left-handed children have been forced to become right-handers. Compelling the children to change hands causes problems. Forcing a left-hander to write using the right hand can have adverse effects in later stages of life. It is traumatic for the child and ruins the legibility of his or her handwriting. Changing the hand used for writing causes great confusion in the brain and can have a lot of negative effects. Natural left-handers should always be allowed to develop in their own way and be allowed to write left-handed if that is their choice.

Biological Functioning

Each side of the brain comprises four lobes:

- The frontal lobe is located at the front of the brain and is associated with reasoning, motor skills, higher level cognition, and expressive language. This area of the brain receives information from various lobes of the brain and utilizes this information to carry out body movements. This lobe is further divided into pre-frontal and post-frontal lobes.

- The parietal lobe is located in the middle section of the brain and is associated with processing tactile sensory information such as pressure, touch, pain and movement.
- The occipital lobe is located at the back portion of the brain and is primarily responsible for vision.

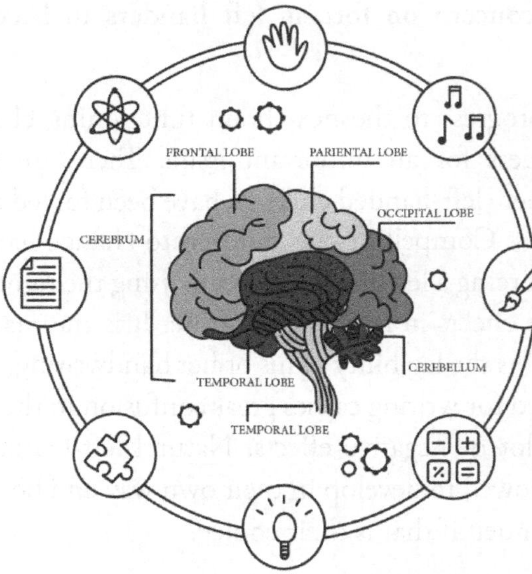

- The temporal lobe processes memories, integrating them with sensations of taste, sound, sight and touch.

There are neural connections between the fingers and the brain lobes in the following manner:

- Thumb and pre-frontal lobe
- Index finger and post-frontal lobe
- Middle finger and parietal lobe
- Ring finger and temporal lobe
- Small finger and occipital lobe

These connections exist in cross section. The left hand fingers are connected to the right side lobes whereas the right hand fingers are connected to the left side lobes of brain.

When a child's fingers work on an abacus in a pre-defined "finger movement" pattern, various lobes of the brain automatically starts to exercise.

Analyse the popular, time tested and effective concept of yogic mudras. Mudras are symbolic gestures often practiced with the hands and fingers. They facilitate the flow of energy in the subtle body and enhance one's journey within.

There are around 12 mudras. However, in context of abacus, we will discuss only Gyan Mudra and Shuni Mudra here.

- **Gyan Mudra:** This mudra involves thumb and index finger. It is the most used mudra while using abacus. Gyan Mudra is known for improving concentration and sharpening the memory.

- **Shuni Mudra:** This mudra, again a common move in abacus, is performed using the middle finger and the thumb. Shuni Mudra is known for improving attention, alertness, and sensory powers.

While working on abacus, the children use their thumbs, index fingers, and middle finger in a predefined finger movement and thus exercising the frontal lobes.

The yogic mudras come into play while a child works on Abacus albeit in a different way.

Chronological Functioning

The brain grows or develops the most in the child's earliest formative years. At the time of birth, the average baby's brain is about 25% the size of an adult's brain. By the time the child reaches the age of 5, it is almost 90%. During this period, the brain is in a relaxed stage or the theta (θ) stage.

In any gathering, the children up to 5-6 years of age are the most relaxed and least concerned participants. They go around shouting, running, playing; they are the least bothered about their appearance or clothes or what others will feel about them. They are fully relaxed.

A new-born child has all the neurons they will have for the rest of their life, but it is the connections between these cells that really make the brain work. Brain connections enable you to move, think, communicate and do just about everything. The early childhood years are crucial for making these connections. At least one million new neural connections (synapses) are made every second, more than at any other time in life.

These initial years of a child are extremely critical. The experiences of this age directly shape the synapses. All positive experiences will have a positive impact on psychological behaviour of child whereas negative experiences will leave a traumatic impact on the child. The learning at this age is more through life experiences rather than formal education system.

As a child grows to be a teenager, the frontal lobe of the child grows which controls his or her decision-making ability. Thus, the child starts moving from Theta (θ) stage to Alpha (α) stage which is relaxed and conscious. The more the child progresses towards the Alpha (α) stage, the more conscious he or she becomes. This also means the formation of synapses starts to slow down as we progress to the end of Alpha (α) stage.

Imagine that there is a wedding, which you want your child to attend. A 4-year child will always oblige whereas a teenager can demand a lot of convincing. This is because they are developing the ability to make decisions. However, they may or may not have experience to make the right decisions and can easily get influenced by their peers while making decisions.

The ability to learn and imagine is plenty at this age. This is the right age for formal learning. The prime age of schooling as well as the correct age for getting the maximum benefits of the abacus program is 5 to 13 years. However, a lot of children of 4-5 years of age are still exiting the relaxed stage for formal sessions.

So, from more of a practical perspective, the suggested age is 6 to 13 years for abacus program.

As children progress towards 20s, the brain activity shifts towards Beta (β) stage and deterioration begins. One may still be able to continue to create and eliminate synapses. But as the age progresses, brain slows down production of brain cells, plus it is not doing as much "pruning"—which is why you have a harder time learning. As we age further, we start to forget things and brain functioning starts to deteriorate.

These neurons draw the analogy to electrical circuits in a house. Let us take an example of a room being constructed and electrical wiring is in progress. There is dedicated wiring to every bulb, tube light or fan from the room's switchboard. The wiring is internal and neatly done. Similarly, the neural synapses that are formed in your body's formative years are neat and control everything cleanly. Once the construction is completed, and then there is a need to add an additional light or a fan, the wiring is usually external and is not as neat as one done during construction phase. Same is true with the brain. The learning is not as clean as it is in the formative years.

What have we learned so far about the brain? The human brain is logically divided into two hemispheres—the left and the right. Each hemisphere has its own sets of functionalities, but they work together. Biologically, there are five clearly defined lobes in both the hemispheres. These are called pre-frontal, post-frontal, parietal, temporal and occipital. There are millions of neurons connecting the five lobes of the left hemisphere of the brain to the five fingers of the right hand of the child and vice versa. The brain tends to grow faster in the initial years. Post 20 years of age, the brain starts to deteriorate. The best learning age is between 6–13 years.

The abacus works as a tool that creates an optimum situation to hone our brain.

4 CHAPTER

ABACUS, THE TOOL

With the knowledge we have, now arises the need of a tool that can help us exercise and stimulate the brain. A tool, which, at the same time can help us evaluate the improvements, qualitatively and quantitatively. A tool that requires the use of the fingers of both hands to stimulate the two halves of the brain in the relevant lobes. A tool that can have academic relevance. A tool that can help provide manifestation for quality assessment of improvement attained in cognitive skills.

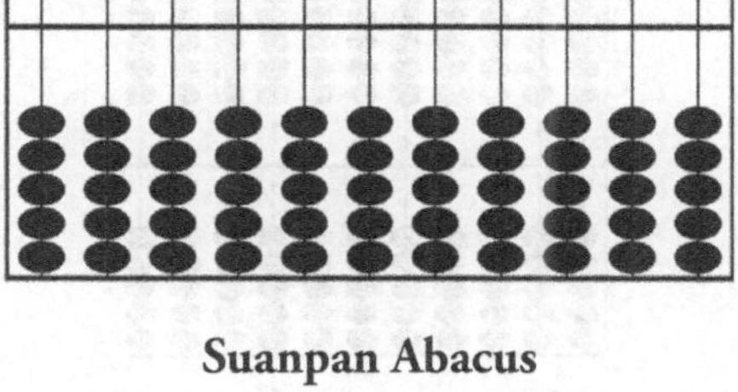

Suanpan Abacus

The tool that fits in all the parameters mentioned above is the Abacus. An abacus is a counting device used to assist a person in performing arithmetic calculations.

The usage of the abacus dates to Mesopotamia in 2700 BC. Gradually, it started to appear in other places as people found it useful in the calculation. In Asia, first the Chinese abacus called Suanpan was developed which became famous globally. From China, the abacus reached Japan, and the Japanese created a more efficient version called the Soroban. In Europe, the Greek, the Roman and the Russian abacus were developed. There are many more varieties of abacus developed over the years across the world. In fact, in the city of Nantong in China, there is a museum dedicated entirely to the abacus, known as the China Nantong Abacus Museum.

Soroban Abacus

Then there is a School abacus which is used in the primary classes to teach counting to young kids.

Originally, abaci (plural for abacus) were made from wood and stones were used as beads.

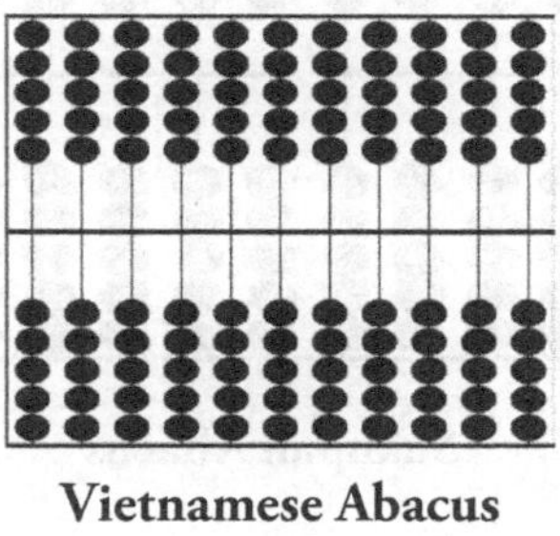

Vietnamese Abacus

It is incredible how people worldwide developed similar devices consisting of beads representing numbers. Simply put, the abacus is the ancestor of the modern-day calculator.

From the abacus program's perspective for cognitive skill enhancement, the most used abacus is the Soroban design. Almost every abacus company in India uses the Soroban.

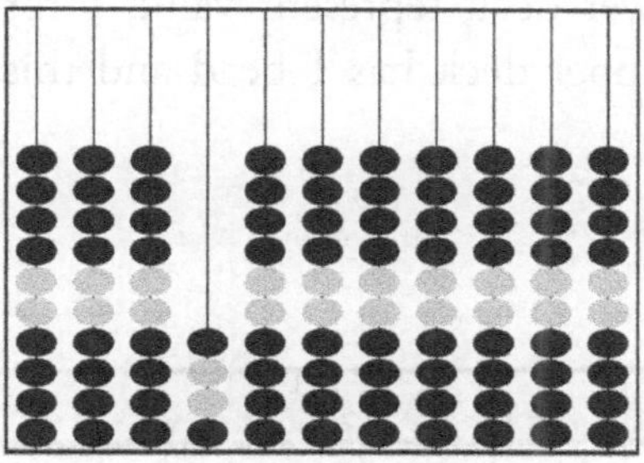

Russian Stschoty Abacus

There are times when people get confused that the standard 10 bead school abacus is used for abacus education. The school abacus is used to explain to little children the concept of numbers and basic addition and subtraction.

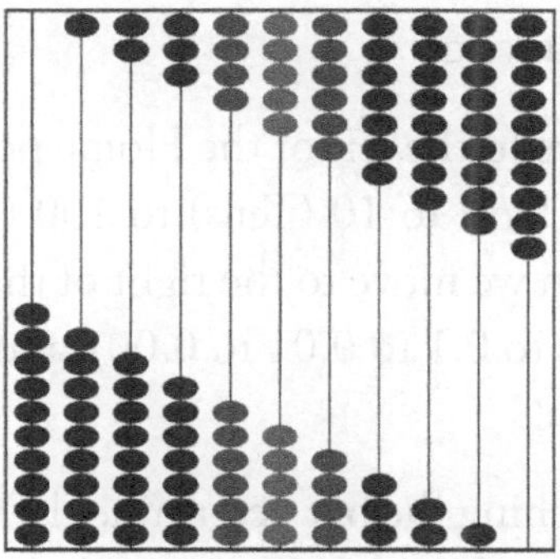

School Abacus

The Soroban design can have 7, 13, 17, 23 or 25 rods. The 17 rod abacus is the most common. Each rod is divided in two parts by a horizontal Beam/Bar. The beads that fall below the bar, constitute the Lower Deck and those beads that are above the bar, constitute the Upper Deck. The centre rod, normally depicted by a dot or a different coloured bead, is called the Unit Point/Home. Each rod has 4 beads in the lower deck. These beads in the lower deck represent value 1 for each bead. For every rod, the upper deck has 1 bead and this bead represents the value 5.

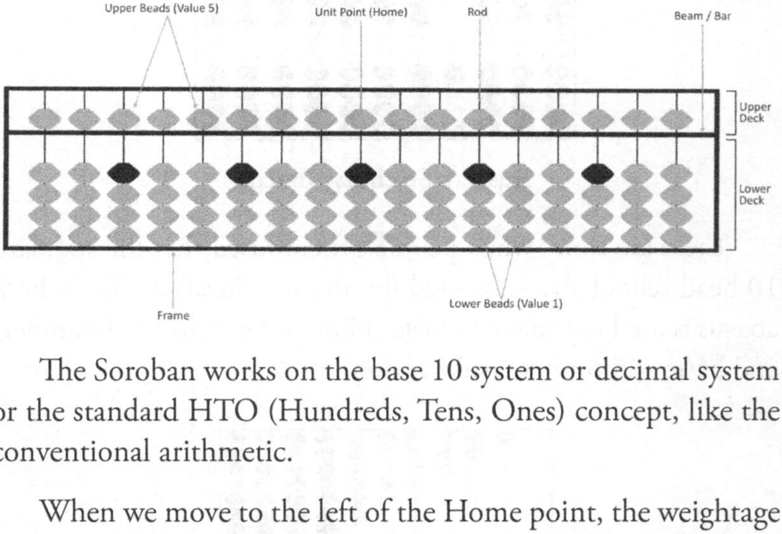

The Soroban works on the base 10 system or decimal system or the standard HTO (Hundreds, Tens, Ones) concept, like the conventional arithmetic.

When we move to the left of the Home point, the weightage changes from 1 (Ones) to 10 (Tens) to 100 (Hundreds) and so on. Similarly, when we move to the right of the Home point, the weightage changes to 0.1 to 0.01 to 0.001 and so on. This is like the decimal system.

The beads touching the bar determine the value of the house. Some examples to indicate the numerical value of the beads in Soroban:

Beads	Value	Explanation
	0	As there is no bead touching the bar on any of the rods, the value of abacus is 0.
	1	Only 1 lower bead (having value 1) is touching the bar on the unit's rod, therefore the value of abacus is 1.
	2	2 lower beads (having value 1 each) are touching the bar on the unit's rod, therefore the value of abacus is 2.
	5	1 upper bead (having value 5) is touching the bar on the unit's rod, therefore the value of abacus is 5.
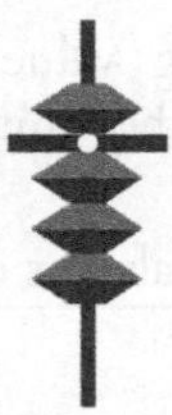	8	1 upper bead (having value 5) & 3 lower beads (having value 1 each) are touching the bar on the unit's rod, therefore the value of abacus is 8.

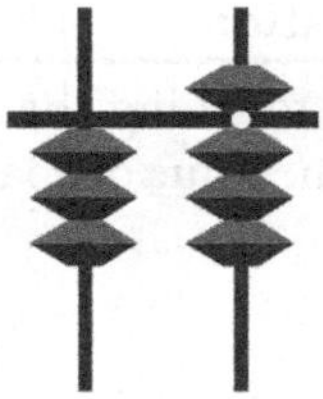	38	3 lower beads (having value 1 each) are touching the bar on the tens' rod, which makes it 30. 1 upper bead (having value 5) & 3 lower beads (having value 1 each) are touching the bar on the unit's rod, which makes it 8. Therefore, the value of abacus is 38.
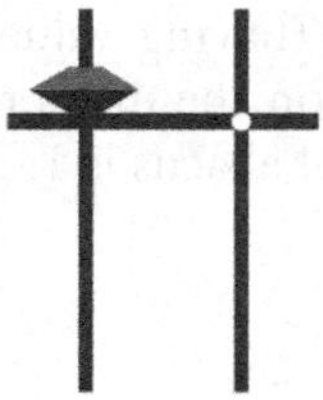	50	1 upper bead (having value 5) is touching the bar on the tens' rod, which makes it 50. No bead is touching the bar on the unit's rod, which makes it 0. Therefore, the value of abacus is 50.
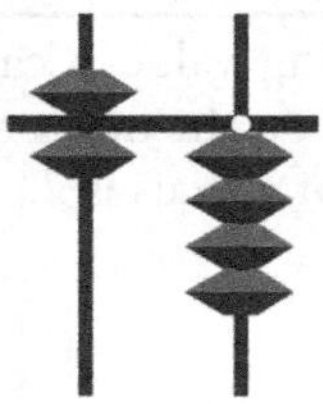	64	1 upper bead (having value 5) & 1 lower bead (having value 1) are touching the bar on the tens' rod, which makes it 60. 4 lower beads (having value 1 each) are touching the bar on the unit rod, which makes it 4. Therefore, the value of abacus is 64.
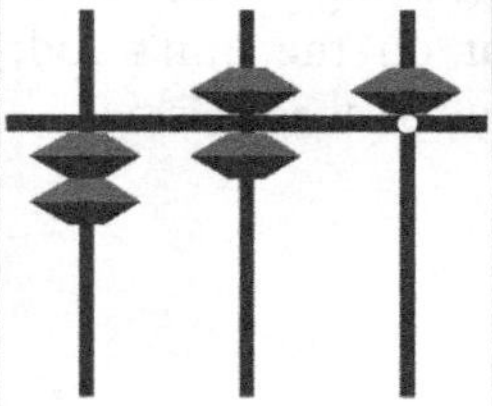	265	2 lower beads (having value 1 each) are touching the bar on the hundreds' rod, which makes it 200. 1 upper bead (having value 5) & 1 lower bead (having value 1) are touching the bar on the tens' rod, which makes it 60. 1 upper bead (having value 5) is touching the bar on the unit's rod, which makes it 5. Therefore, the value of abacus is 265.

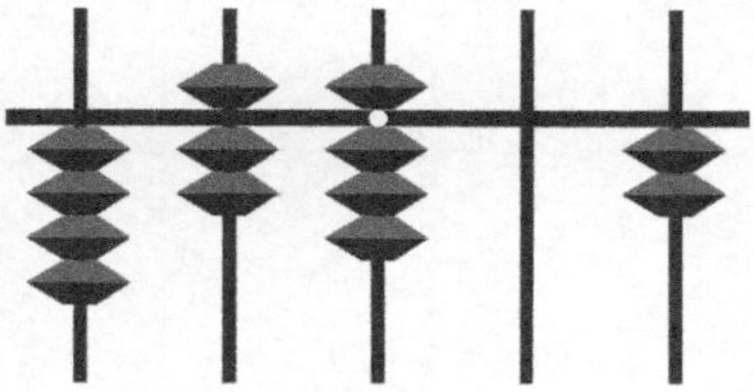	478.02	4 lower beads (having value 1 each) are touching the bar on the hundreds' rod, which makes it 400. 1 upper bead (having value 5) & 2 lower beads (having value 1 each) are touching the bar on the tens' rod, which makes it 70. 1 upper bead (having value 5) & 3 lower beads (having value 1 each) are touching the bar on the unit's rod, which makes it 8. No bead is touching the bar on the 1/10 (0.1) rod, which makes it 0. 2 lower beads (having value 1 each) are touching the bar on the 1/100 (0.01) rod, which makes it 0.02. Therefore, the value of abacus is 478.02.

CHAPTER 5

ROLE OF ARITHMETIC

The role of arithmetic in the abacus program has three facets. They are:

1. Medium of practice
2. Assessment criterion of improvement
3. Convincing necessity

The first facet is a logical conclusion of the fact, that abacus, the tool used to exercise our brain, is a counting device. The questions or problems that need to be solved on the abacus, must be arithmetical.

A small trivia! What is the difference between arithmetic and mathematics?

Arithmetic

1. the branch of mathematics that deals with addition, subtraction, multiplication, and division

2. the use of numbers in calculations

Mathematics

1. the study of the relationships among numbers, shapes, and quantities,
2. it uses signs, symbols, and proofs and includes arithmetic, algebra, calculus, geometry, and trigonometry.

Arithmetic is a subset of mathematics and in abacus, we remain restricted to arithmetic only.

Arithmetic is independent of the spoken or local language. The instructor can deliver the class in the language in which the students are comfortable. It can be English, Hindi, or any language for that matter. It is important that the child understands the conept.

In the abacus program, general practice followed by various institutes is to divide the entire curriculum or course structure into 8 to 10 levels. Generally, each level is of 3-4 months and the program continues for about 2 to 3 years depending upon the structure. The length or the duration of the program does not indicate the quality of program. It is more about how the course has been structured.

Every child irrespective of age begins the abacus program by first doing addition, then progressing to subtraction, multiplication, division and then combination of these, in the same order. The course structure of the abacus program is not meant to focus on learning these basic arithmetic concepts in the classes. It is assumed that a child is already learning them in the formal school and is aware of these concepts. Rather, the focus is on implementation of these concepts on the abacus.

When you prepare for a long race of say 10 kilometres, you prepare for it gradually. On day 1, you would start from running, may be say 500 metres in 10 minutes. Then gradually, with every passing day, you increase the running distance towards your target of 10 kilometres by increasing your physical stamina and at the same time reducing the time taken to run the same distance by increasing your speed. The timelines to achieve the target will vary from individual to individual. The same person at two different stages of life, at different fitness levels, will have two different timelines.

Similarly, as we progress from one level to another in an abacus program, the complexity of arithmetic questions increases. The target is to make the questions more complex and reduce the time taken to solve these questions. As the questions become bigger and more complex, the calculation involved increases. As the calculation increases, the number of finger movements required to solve the question also increases accordingly. As the finger movement increases the brain stimulation increases and so on. As far as the scale of improvement is concerned, the sky is the limit. The more a student practices, the better results can be achieved, and the mental arithmetic results can be very impressive.

As in the case of the race, we defined the progress in terms of length one could run on that day. Similarly, in abacus, the progress of a child is defined in terms of difficulty of the arithmetic question, the size of the expression and the time taken to solve the arithmetic question.

In a mathematical expression 3 + 6, the "3" and "6" are the operands and "+" is the operator. So, as the child progresses in the program, the total number of operands, as well as the value of the operands begins to increase.

A common notation to symbolize the size of the expression is digits and rows. Digits represent the number of digits in operand, whereas rows, represents total number of operands.

Example:

Add:	3, 5, 1, 9, 7	→1 digit 5 rows
Add:	78, -35, 16, 48, -33, 58, 28	→2 digits 7 rows
Add:	650, 746, - 406, 332	→3 digits 4 rows
Multiply:	754 x 39	→3 digits x 2 digits

As a child progresses from one level to another, the challenge increases in terms of digits, rows and time taken to solve the question.

An important query from parents arises quite often: "Since the child practices so much on the abacus, must he or she carry the abacus along for life?"

The answer is "No". As children progress, they form the image of the abacus and the beads in their brain's right hemispheres and are able to visualize the movement of the beads without needing the physical tool. As the children start with single-digit questions, they do them on abacus. Gradually as they progress to double digits, they start developing the image of abacus and begin to solve the single-digit questions mentally. The same trend continues as they progress from 2 to 3 digits and more. This is one reason why abacus program is also referred to as both an abacus and mental arithmetic system.

The next facet is the assessment criterion. Cognitive skills are relative skills and it may not be easy to measure them objectively. We have understood that concentration or processing speed is one of the cognitive skills that improve with the abacus program. But what is good for one child may be average for others. There is no way to measure concentration. We cannot say if the concentration of the child is 2 kg or 5 kg. How do we assess if the child's concentration skill has improved as he or she undergoes the abacus program? Arithmetic again comes to rescue.

Let us take the example of an arithmetic question, that requires to add ten numbers (2 digits, 10 rows' addition). Generally, an average student may solve it in about 60 seconds whereas a child who performs above average can solve the same question in about 45 seconds. However, if these children can solve them in 2-3 seconds or say even in 10 seconds, the improvement is obvious and quantifiable.

Imagine, solving a similar question, in two ways. First, where the question is written on a piece of paper and the student must solve it. Second, where these 10 numbers are being read out and needs to be solved without any pen or paper. Which is easy? The former requires arithmetic skills, whereas the latter in addition to arithmetic skills, requires a gamut of cognitive skills. Solving a question by auditory means requires listening skills, concentration, comprehension, memory and processing speed, because if even one number is missed, the answer is bound to be wrong. So, when the children are made to solve big arithmetic questions without pen and paper, their cognitive skills are being tested.

Have you ever seen a detergent's advertisement? Generally, the advertisement focuses on problem, the "stains", and then the brand being advertised is projected to clean those stains. The brands would sweeten the deal by talking about add-ons like fragrance, packaging, offers, environmental friendliness, etc.

When it comes to cars, the relevant car brands talk about features like mileage, styling, safety, speed, seating and luggage space. They focus on features and enhance the deal by adding payment options, exchange offers, loyalty bonuses, and more such offers.

Similarly, when the parents want to know the convincing reasons why and how the abacus program is beneficial for their children, the abacus institutes address the core issues like mathematics phobia, the child's ability to calculate faster than the calculator, and so on.

But, in the case of detergent and cars, people are aware of their usage and need. The brands do not need to convince the buyers that they need to buy soaps or cars. People will buy them anyway, if they need them. They just need to convince the customers to buy their brand over the others.

But in case of abacus, the companies need to convince the parents of the importance of abacus education first. Explaining about the abacus program with so much technical content, is a gargantuan challenge for an advertising professional.

But more than these sales pitches, it is the demonstration of the arithmetic skills of the children that is more effective in communicating the message. Watching these kids whip through complicated sums leave most adults slack-jawed. This admiration is a dramatic solution, given most parents themselves have a fear of mathematics!

So, at the end of day, the program delivers more than what was promised. The promise is excellent math skills. The delivery, however, is that, in addition to overcoming any fear of math:

- Kids learn to be able to calculate astonishing sums unassisted in seconds

- They overcome any fear of calculating under pressure and with an audience (another fear most adults harbour)
- Kids can see a direct link between their practice and improved results, giving them a work ethic that is useful throughout one's life
- They develop confidence and poise in their skills and ability to learn and grow
- And in general, you can expect development and improvement in your child's overall performance.

Any complaints?

6 CHAPTER

THE RIGHT APPROACH

Now that we have understood the basics that go behind the abacus program, we will discuss the best practices, right approach, and various dos & don'ts; when you implement it accordingly, the abacus program will be highly effective.

1. Consistent and Daily Practice

There is an old saying:

40 days: To change or break a habit.

90 days: To confirm a new habit.

120 days: The new habit is who you are.

1000 days: You have mastered the new habit.

This is simply because our brain does not accept a change unless we keep repeating it. Any change in our body is effective and everlasting if it is gradual and consistent.

Consider a person who wishes to be healthy & fit. He or she decides to go for a 2 km morning walk every day. This morning walk will only be effective and helpful if the person does it regularly as part of a routine. If he or she decides to walk 15 km once in a week or occasionally, their body will take it as a task. It will just cause temporary energy drain and pain in the legs.

Similarly, when a child is learning abacus, he or she should practice daily for about 10–15 minutes. Generally, the scheduled classes in the centres are held once a week for two hours. There is always some homework given to a child. It is a good practice to divide the same into 5-6 parts and do one part daily for 6 days during the break between the two consecutive classes. Abacus institutes should also try to plan the homework so that children can practice regularly at home.

Sometimes, situations like holidays or the child falling sick on the scheduled day of class lead to prolonged gap between the two classes. This causes a longer than anticipated or planned gap between two classes. The parents should get in touch with the respective teachers or centre-in-charges to reschedule the classes in as much advance as possible. This will help to minimize the gap. A good institute generally keeps a slot for such contingencies. Although provisioning these slots are never obligatory on the centre and is generally done on the best effort basis.

It is always a good practice for the parents to act as facilitators and help their children practice at home. When the parents get involved in practice sessions, it leads to manifold benefits:

- The children get to practice in an appropriate manner which in turn improves the performance and subsequently the results.

- In case of missed or delayed classes, children do not have a setback as they stay in practice.
- The parents get involved in the learning process of the child. This makes them an effective participant in the learning process.

There are some online computer based apps and tools available like Visual Calculator (www.visualcalculator.in) which can help children practice at home with ease and convenience. Tools like these come very handy for children to improve significantly and it is really a boon to those children who wish to go that extra mile, which makes them a performer and subsequently a winner. These tools come to the rescue of those parents as well, who because of various reasons, are not able to dedicate time or help their children with practice.

Daily practice is of utmost importance. The success of the entire abacus program depends on this very facet. A common question we hear parents asking is, "Will we see improvement in our child after going through the abacus program?" The answer to this question is, "If the child is regular and practices religiously, the results will surely be positive."

2. No Fast Track

During summer vacations, the newspapers carry a lot of flyers and pamphlets offering 15 to 30 days fast track course on the abacus. Parents are advised not to fall into such traps. The cognitive skills develop when the brain is exercised. No quick fix exercise gives you results instantly.

When a doctor prescribes medicine for an ailment thrice a day for five days, the body will accept the medicine as a remedy for the discomfort or ailment if the medicine is taken as per the schedule and for the complete course. To save time and effort, we cannot replace the complete course of 5 days by taking 15 tablets at once. Rest assured, it will be very harmful due to drug overdose rather than any medicinal benefit.

Similar situation is with the abacus as well. For exercising the brain, the effort must be consistent and persistent. Rushing through a fast-track abacus program will be an overdose of concept with zero exercise of the brain. Children may be able to learn a few concepts of abacus but the improvements pertaining to cognitive skills may not happen.

3. Avoid use of Erasers/Mark the Wrong Questions

It is strongly advised to avoid the use of erasers in class while attempting an arithmetic question. The idea of this process is to identify the grey areas and improve accuracy. Alternately, if the students use the erasers, they should circle the questions that were wrong in the first attempt.

  2
+3
~~4~~ 5

While writing an exam it is particularly important that the accuracy must be high, and questions are answered correctly in the first attempt. There is no certainty if a child will get time to revise at the end of an examination. So, if the child is able to write the answers correctly with high accuracy, the performance and the result will be better.

When children make a mistake, they should strike the incorrect answer and write the correct answer next to it.

Therefore, avoiding eraser or marking the question, will highlight their mistakes and weakness. This gives the teacher or educator a glimpse to the weak areas of a child. If a child is making frequent mistakes in solving similar questions, the teacher can take cognizance of the same. The teacher can then work on these areas to ensure that all concepts are thoroughly understood by the children.

4. Competitions

Several abacus institutes organize abacus and mental arithmetic competitions at various levels - city, regional, state, national or international levels.

These competitions give challenging tasks to the children like solving 100-200 questions in 5 to 10 minutes. Though, this may sound impossible to many but for the children who are undergoing the abacus training, this is very much doable.

The competitions are done with a lot of fanfare, therefore participation in these motivate the children to prepare and practice. There is only one champion in any competition, but every participant is a winner. The winning or biggest takeaway for every child is the quantum of improvement that happens when a child practices during the run-up for the event.

The second takeaway is the exposure. A child, in a normal circumstance, gets to compete with his or her classmates only. Excelling in the class is relatively easy, but when a child prepares to participate at state or national level, his or her performance can leapfrog previous levels. The children realize their true potential. The exposure at a young age comes very handy, when the child grows up to face the real life and the whole world is the competition.

When these competitions are organized by a company in closed user group, the competition is organized amongst the peers who are at the same level of course. For example, students at Level 1 participate against the students of Level 1. So, the result is fair and square.

However, at times, a lot of event companies, announce open competitions, where anyone can participate. In these competitions, children participate in self-declared levels. It is exceedingly difficult to judge the authenticity of such declarations and children meant to compete in higher levels participate in lower levels to win the competition, and the result would always comes in their favour. Participation in such events can be avoided.

5. Interaction of Parents–Teachers–Centre-In-Charge

A good abacus centre or company will always facilitate the interaction between parents, teachers and centre-in-charge. If the centres do not facilitate this interaction, the parents should insist on it.

The first interaction happens during the registration of the children. This is referred to as counselling. During this interaction, the centre should introduce the abacus program in detail to the parents—what is abacus program, how does it help the child, what are the different benchmarks, course structure, course material, process, events, facilities the centre offers, and most importantly, set the expectations of the course right.

The second interaction should happen within one month of the student joining the program. This interaction should focus on the basics of the abacus program. This is an important session. The parents are expected to help their children with homework and home practice. However, without basic knowledge of the program, the parents will not be able to actively participate in the process. If the parents are introduced to the basic information like reading the values on abacus, various formulae used, etc., the parents can be active participant in their child's development.

Other than these, the parents and the teacher should meet once in a month or at least twice in a quarter to get regular updates on the child's performance and should discuss what actions should be taken in case the child's performance is not up to the mark, or if there is any deviation from the expected path.

6. Parent's Support

Parent's support starts from the day the children are born. As children grow from infancy to adulthood, they require tremendous support from their parents for their physical, emotional, social, spiritual and intellectual development.

Same applies for abacus also. For the success of the program, the parents need to ensure these practices.

- Be a well-informed parent. Know about the program and the progress of the child. Keep in regular touch with the teachers to get feedback and take corrective steps if necessary.
- Abacus needs to be practiced daily. As a parent, dedicate some time to the child's practice.
- Maintain good balance between school education and non-school education. Give equal importance to other programs like abacus, co-curricular, music, sports, etc. The school marks have never been an indicator of the child's success.
- Please avoid comparing your child with other children.

- Never pressurize your child to win, but always insist as well as motivate your child to prepare.
- No single examination makes or breaks a child's future. Always have a plan B in case the child fails in one avenue.
- Be a friend of your child. As the children grow, they start confiding in their friends, because there is no fear of being reprimanded. However, the friends may not be the best person for advice or guidance due to their inexperience in life. So, if children can find a friend, in their parents, they will always be well guided.
- Try to appreciate your child in public but ensure that you never criticise them in front of anyone. Praising the child's effort in public encourages the child to always keep trying. Public criticism is humiliating and discourages him or her.

7. Celebrate Milestones

It should not be about just learning; rejoicing should also follow every successful learning. If your child achieves something ordinary or valuable, every successful attempt in the learning of abacus should be acknowledged and rewarded. This practice to incentivize your kids will help them to understand abacus with greater enthusiasm, which in turn will enhance their interest in the program and subsequently your child will emerge as a good student of abacus learning.

CHAPTER 7

FREQUENTLY ASKED QUESTIONS

Q1. What is the difference between abacus program and vedic mathematics? Which is better?

An abacus program is a cognitive skill enhancement program which uses abacus as a tool and arithmetic as a medium to learn and helps children perform better in all aspects of life. It is meant for children of 6-13 years age group.

Vedic mathematics is an ancient Indian methodology based on 16 shlokas or sutras and 13 sub sutras that help to solve complex mathematics based on arithmetic, algebra, geometry, calculus and conics with ease.

Vedic mathematics is a powerful concept, but its use is selective and situational. Some of the concepts are not universal when applied. It means a method X is applicable for questions that uses specific numbers. If these number changes, the same method may not be applicable.

It is difficult to explain the selective methodology to younger children, as it can confuse them. Some of the topics like calculus covered in Vedic maths are meant for older students. Therefore, Vedic mathematics is helpful for children who are in higher classes (class VIII or above).

Both programs have a different purpose and are meant for different age groups. So, when it comes to selecting the program for your child, selection should be based on age and purpose of learning.

Q2. Once my children are habituated of using abacus, will they need to carry the abacus with them throughout their life to be able to solve the arithmetic questions?

Once children are habituated of using the abacus, they form its image in their right brain. They can solve the arithmetic questions mentally and therefore do not require carrying the abacus throughout their life.

Q3. What happens after the child completes this program? How will he or she continue to practice and use whatever was learned during the program?

Arithmetic finds its usage in almost every field and phase of life. Once a child has completed the program, he or she will be using arithmetic all his or her life and in turn, will get to practice what he or she has learned.

Q4. Will my child get confused while solving an arithmetic question, as there is a difference in the method followed by abacus classes and that of school?

The only way to teach numbers is through counting. There is no other way. We count various objects while explaining the numbers to young kids. While learning numbers on an abacus, our objects are the beads. The Soroban abacus uses the standard concepts of Number lines system and Decimal system (HTO system) as taught in schools. So, the method used in abacus or in schools is virtually the same, only the objects have changed. So, the children will not get confused.

Q5. Why do we have class once a week? Why cannot we have more than one classes of smaller duration?

There are two reasons why the classes are held once a week.

1. Abacus program is experiential in nature. When any concept is introduced, in the class, several activities are conducted to ensure better understanding and grasping of that concept. These activities are time-consuming. Classes having lesser duration will split these activities across classes making them less effective.

   Assume a cooking class. If you are teaching to make a dish, which takes an hour and a half to prepare, we would need the same time for the class. We cannot do half preparation on day one and remaining preparation in next class.

2. Logistic comfort is another reason, although not very significant. The abacus classes are meant for 6-13 years old children who are school going. The classes therefore need to be conducted in non-school hours, generally over the weekend. Parents would need to arrange for a pick-up and drop multiple times in a week, which will be wastage of time and money both.

Q6. If my child can grasp the concepts faster, can the program be finished earlier? Can we fast-track the programs?

For exercising the brain, the effort must be consistent and persistent. Rushing through a fast-track abacus program will be overdose of concept with zero exercise of the brain. Although the child may be able to grasp the concept faster, but the cognitive skills will still require time to develop. Finishing the program quickly, may not give better or desired results.

Q7. Why is daily practice important?

Daily practice is of utmost importance. The success of the entire abacus program depends on this very facet. Brain does not accept a change unless it receives the same message repeatedly. Any change in our body is effective and everlasting if it is gradual and consistent. Therefore, daily practice is a must.

Q8. My child studies in a school which promotes abacus classes. How is it different from private centres?

Abacus program in most of the schools is run as just another activity where not much importance or seriousness is accorded. The result is that the parents and students do not take it seriously and are hardly regular. Like sports, music or any other co-curricular activities, the classes are frequently cancelled or replaced as per academic priorities.

Abacus is interesting and fun-filled learning but needs serious attention and practice.

The private centres ensure that the due seriousness is warranted, and they work hard to achieve the purpose.

Abacus program in school can only be successful if the school gives the necessary academic weightage to it.

Q9. What should I do if my child misses a class due to personal engagement?

Missing 1 or 2 classes every 6 months is manageable. However, every missed class creates a gap. The parents should talk to the teacher or centre-in-charge to arrange for a makeover class. If the absence is planned, the makeover class should be requested in advance. If the absence is unplanned, it should be requested as soon as the engagement is over. However, the parents should make effort to ensure that the practice continues uninterruptedly.

Q10. Due to medical reasons (or for any other reason), my child will miss multiple classes. What should be my approach?

In an unfortunate event of medical emergency or any unspecified emergency which causes absence in multiple or continuous classes, the parents should meet the centre-in-charge and arrange transfer of the student to the next batches. Also, the parents can request practice material from the centre to ensure that the child maintains in continuity.

Q11. I am moving to a new city. The company where my child goes to study currently does not have a centre there. What is the best approach I should take?

A lot of abacus companies allow transfer of students from one centre to another. However, if the new city does not have the centre from existing company, parents could request transfer to another company's centres. For smooth transfer, the parents should retain the existing fee receipts, certificates issued after every level by the current centre.

Considering that all companies follow their own course structure, the level at a new centre may differ on the basis of what child knows and where does that fits in the structure.

Q12. How is the abacus used for cognitive skills enhancement different from the play school abacus?

The abacus used in play school, is merely a counting device and is used to teach the concept of numbers to the children. The abacus used for cognitive skill enhancement program facilitates exercise of the brain.

Q13. While using abacus, does it matter if my child is left-handed?

It does not matter if the child is right-handed or left-handed as far as the outcome is concerned. There may be a slight difference in the technique or way the fingers are moved on the abacus. A good teacher would be capable to guide the student accordingly.

CHAPTER 8

THE 8 LEARNING STYLES

According to Howard Gardner, Harvard professor of cognition and education, everybody has different learning styles to comprehend new information; this is the "Theory of Multiple Intelligences."

While designing the learning pedagogy of a good abacus program, it is imperative that, the created learning aids cover the needs of students with assorted learning styles.

It is important to have a good understanding of each of these types of learning styles for teachers as well as parents so that they can help the children get the most out of the class or home study.

1. Visual or Spatial Learner

Visual or spatial learners require images, diagrams, or graphs to understand and retain information. These pictures help these children in guiding them through the learning process. A picture speaks a thousand words to these children. They find concepts making sense more readily when presented visually.

Visual learners tend to veer towards technology-driven careers, as well as industries related to art, photography, architecture and design. They have vivid imaginations and are often good at coming up with unusual or unexpected ways to solve problems.

The use of flash cards in abacus program helps spatial learners, as it depicts the numbers as images.

2. Reading/Writing, Linguistic, or Verbal Learner

Linguistic or verbal learners absorb information through reading, writing, listening and speaking. They prefer to make their own notes and create their own information bank. They highlight, edit and rewrite important points in their notes. Such students also prefer solving previous examination papers and multiple choice questions. They have a fascination for vocabulary and tend to learn new words almost effortlessly. As a result, they have a rich vocabulary. They tend to do better with word problems in maths in comparison to equations. The linguistic learners like to talk about what they read and remember rhymes, quotes easily.

Verbal learners often have an excellent memory and are likely to become teachers or professors.

The use of speed writing in an abacus program helps linguistic learners excel.

3. Auditory, Aural or Musical Learner

If these kids are not listening, they are not learning. These kids love to listen. They pay attention to the tone, pitch and volume of the teacher in class and prefer audio recordings of lessons to get clarity. Combine the audio recording with music and be surprised by your child's attention level. Auditory or musical learning circles around sound, music, and rhythm to help retain information.

Music learners prefer spoken directions, find it difficult to concentrate in noisy environments, and remember names, not faces.

These types of learners often become musicians as they have a deeper understanding of music.

Auditory or aural exercises are an integral part of an Abacus Program and these not only help improve the listening skills of a child but also help the aural listener with his or her learning abilities.

4. Kinaesthetic or Physical Learner

Kinaesthetic learners cannot seem to sit still. They learn quickly and permanently through what they do.

Tell these kids to read or write about a concept, they won't be interested. But involve them in projects, demonstrations, or role plays of the same concept and see the spike in their enthusiasm level. Kinaesthetic or physical learning requires the learners to be hands-on to understand the process and retain information.

Kinaesthetic learners love artsy, creative, or athletic careers, and will often choose activities such as jewellery-making, gardening and woodworking as hobbies.

Core to an abacus program is using an abacus, a kinaesthetic activity!

5. Logical or Mathematical Learner

Logical learners look for patterns and shapes in the world around them. They cannot blindly memorise a term. They love logical examples or statistics to help them understand a complicated problem. If they know the logic behind a mathematical equation, they can even surprise you by solving a complex calculation manually.

People with logical or mathematical learning styles use reasoning and logical sequencing to absorb information. Their strengths are in math, logic, seeing patterns and problem-solving. They like to work with numbers, find logical methods to answer questions, classify, and categorize. They are comfortable working with the abstract.

Logical learners tend to go on to be engineers, mathematicians and scientists, and are often exceptionally good at playing strategy games like chess and backgammon.

One of the practice methodologies in the abacus is Basic Exercises, which requires repetitive addition of numbers in a defined fashion. These exercises help children who are logical learners.

6. Intrapersonal or Solitary Learner

Intrapersonal or solitary learning include people who learn and work best on their own. They are very introspective and reflective. They prefer to sit alone and focus their thoughts on the topic at hand.

They usually keep a journal or diary, enjoy spending time alone, like to set goals and make plans, have a strong sense of self, and are endowed with excellent self-management skills

They are very independent and prefer positions without direct leadership or supervision.

Intrapersonal learners are likely to enter creative fields and even become entrepreneurs or small-business owners.

7. Interpersonal or Social Learner

Interpersonal or social learning means this type of learner performs best when they're able to relate to others and work in groups. They learn to study in groups and love talking to others to get clarity. They even prefer spending a lot of one-on-one time with teachers.

These learners need to be able to bounce ideas off others and interact with others. They are much better at reading emotions and facial expressions and are often extroverts. They like to hang out with large groups of people and do well with study groups. Social learners are not afraid to ask questions and enjoy taking part in social activities. They make new friends quickly.

Interpersonal learners might become psychologists or social workers and enjoy positions where they're working with people.

8. Naturalistic Learner

Naturalistic learning focuses on the need to be outside in nature to guide the learning process. These types of learners prefer to be out of doors, observing how things work in nature. Unsurprisingly, those with this learning style often end up becoming scientists or horticulturists.

The naturalistic learners can make unique distinctions in the world of nature. They thrive in environments where they're allowed to feel things and be active participants in activities. They love outdoors and prefer hands-on experiences.

We can connect with naturalistic learners by offering one-on-one sessions outside or allow students to work outside regularly.

CHAPTER 9

THE RIGHT CENTRE

Today's parents have numerous choices, when it comes to selecting the abacus centre for their child. But the penchant for myriad choices leads to confusion, considering mind-boggling promises and jargons used by the centres to promote themselves.

The aspiring individuals who want to explore the opportunity to be an entrepreneur also struggle to decide if they need to start on their own or take up a franchise.

There are no ratings or scales available to suggest the right options. But there are various aspects that one can ponder before taking the final plunge and arriving at a conclusion on selection. These aspects broadly remain the same for parents and budding entrepreneurs.

A franchisee centre is generally a better choice than a standalone centre if your risk appetite is low or you have limited resources, or a nominal exposure to the subject. It is not that stand-alone centres do not perform, but the franchisee centres offer added advantages that play well when it comes to sustainability and offerings. Selection amongst a plethora of franchisees too is a challenge, especially, when it is difficult to differentiate between apropos and malapropos players.

The statistics prove that franchise centres are more stable and long-term sustainable. Most new businesses fail within the first three years of inception. These failures are generally due to one or many reasons such as paucity of knowledge of the product as well as that of the market, a deficit of brand awareness, inept financial planning, or scant resources.

On the contrary, franchising offers a set of proven business structures for entrepreneurs with the strength of national brand names. A franchising organization combines the drive and ambition of independent entrepreneurs with their experience, expertise and proven success formula. The result tends to be rewarding for franchisees and franchisors with increased reach, market penetration, brand equity, growth and revenue potential. In today's economy, franchise systems continue to provide the widest possible entrepreneurial opportunities.

If a standalone centre falters for whatever reasons, the students are left hanging in the lurch. It will be a waste of time and money both. Parents will have to restart the exercise of identifying a new centre. Transition discomfort will be extra. However, in case of franchise centre, the franchisor will ensure an alternate measure to counter the same. They will appoint a new franchisee or delegate the students to a nearby centre. This will ensure that continuity of the program and the interest of the children remains protected.

Franchisors are generally able to offer consistency across their service. They can establish standard operating procedures and guidelines, which are widely accepted. Franchisors make continuous efforts to increase their centre's presence and expand their network. This provides an advantage to the parents in terms of consistent quality and good service near their residences. The consistency is maintained even if they change their house or relocate to a new city.

Another factor that goes in favour of the franchisee centre is the availability of numerous skilled and qualified human resources to customize and improvise the course material vis-à-vis to standalone centres. The abacus books or course material is generally not available in open market. There is no board or regulator specifying the syllabus. Whatever course material needs to be designed or used, it has to be in house. It is difficult for a standalone centre to customize or improvise the course material because of over dependence on the key person for everything. Volume plays an important role in keeping the costs down when it comes to printing. Printing of course material in good quality and quantity, keeping the prices on the lower side, will always be a challenge for the standalone centres. By the virtue of the network, volumes are available to the franchisors, and they can as per the need, ensure implementation of changes and upgrades as well as reprint the new editions keeping the costing in check.

The biggest role in the performance of a centre is that of a teacher. A teacher or a course instructor or an educator, are responsible for final delivery of the program to the students. They can make a bad program look good and make an excellent program look bad. The influence that a good teacher has on the students is everlasting. They know how to bring out the best in the child. Therefore, it is imperative that the teacher is technically and conceptually strong while delivering her sessions. They need to have good interpersonal skills to motivate the children and retain their interests. Interpersonal skills are generally inherent to an individual, but technical skills need to be acquired. To ensure relevant technical skills, a teacher needs to take methodical and relevant training. The teachers must apprise themselves regularly of updated content through refresher session exposure to various forums to collaborate with their peers on best practices and issue resolution.

A good franchisor will always focus stringently on teacher's training. This generally will lack in stand-alone centres. This is also the major differentiator when it comes to identifying the right franchisor.

Competitions and events have always been an integral part of abacus education. The franchisee centres can organize these competitions on an unprecedented scale and in a transparent manner. The standalone centres can arrange, but the standard and scale will nowhere be comparable. Open-for-all competitions cannot be fair as the organizers are dependent on information from participating centres which cannot be verified.

The use of technology is now inexorable. Then why should an abacus centre be devoid of the same? A good franchisor would invest in various tools like a learning management system, ERP system for centre administration, digital course material and student practice tools. These systems help improve productivity, better learning curve for the students, performance bar, smooth management of centre, a better use of time through optimisation.

Parents can review these parameters and arrive at a conclusion identifying the right centre for their child.

CHAPTER 10

A GREAT SELF EMPLOYMENT OPPORTUNITY

Setting up and running an abacus education centre is an excellent self-employment opportunity. The only condition is to do it right, with sincerity and diligence. Education is a noble profession. One must be selfless and always be ready to go all out to assist their students. A successful abacus centre helps in developing a sense of achievement, builds up self-esteem and generates a regular and respectable income. Being in a teaching profession earns you a lot of respect amongst peers, children and parents. It gives you strong social visibility. It instills a sense of pride when your students start performing and showing results.

Abacus centres are generally a part-time affair

We now know that an abacus program is for children of 5-13 years' age group. These students are school going and are generally open for non-school programs like Abacus, either on the weekends or in the evenings. Abacus program requires about two hours per week from every student. These hours are generally allocated over the weekend when the children are available or at times in the evenings of working days. Hence, the time requirement for running an abacus centre is generally concentrated over the weekends.

As the abacus centres run primarily over the weekend, it is suitable for homemakers, retirees, teachers and educationists, who wish to manage their personal and professional life with a lot of comfort and flexibility. Infact, it also offers a win-win situation to numerous play schools that have their premises lying idle over the weekends. It can help offset the real estate costs of such entities.

Abacus education has been immensely popular among the ladies. Women run over 90% of the abacus centres in India, and almost a similar percentage of it is applicable when it comes to educators who are training the children. Thus, abacus education centres have been a strong tool or means for women empowerment and self-sustenance. This, in no way, undermines the contribution of the male counterparts. They too have been successfully running the show. Just that their numbers are fewer. Even if we observe the scenario in the formal school, teaching has largely been a forte of the ladies in the formative years. The number of female teachers far exceeds the male teachers in formal schools.

Typically, Indian women have largely been expected to manage their home affairs. Their upbringing is generally focused on developing skills that would eventually help them manage the household chores. Many girls need to fight their way out to get permission to seek admission in colleges that impart professional education. The ones who manage to be professionally ready and attain thriving careers eventually give up their careers, post marriage, to accommodate the requirement of supporting their family and raising their kids. A corporate job or full-fledged regular business requires long working hours throughout the week. Managing the professional and personal life together mostly complicates things and takes its toll on the lady's physical, mental, social, and emotional state. The women, thus, end up sacrificing their career. Therefore, setting up an abacus centre or seeking a career in abacus education is a great option for them to strike a balance.

Several individuals use abacus centres as an opportunity for a second or additional source of income. People take up regular jobs in corporates or schools over the weekdays and run an abacus institute over the weekend. There are a lot of examples of individuals who have taken up abacus as a part-time profession and gradually outdone their own expectations and have now made it their sole business.

Initial investment makes an abacus education centre even more attractive. Unlike any other business, the requirement of initial capital is miniscule. The gestation period too is surprisingly small. A good centre can recover its investment in about 6-7 months. This is very small when compared to any other options. The requirement of infrastructure is very reasonable. The abacus centre can be run from the convenience of your home as well as renting out a few classrooms at a play school nearby.

The availability of numerous franchisee options makes it easy for one to take a plunge. Past educational or operational experience does not matter much when it comes to running an abacus centre. A good franchisor will provide you with all the necessary technical and administrative training to run the show.

However, one must be careful of the free service providers. Nothing in this world comes for free. A lot of advertisements float around, offering a free abacus franchise. No company can serve you for free. Either there are hidden costs, or these are gimmicks to lure you into the trap to pay heavily later. These free sellers generally make quick bucks by luring you and then suddenly disappear.

Education is one sector which can never be out of favour. The children require ample opportunities and platforms to polish their skills. We have already learned that abacus education helps the children prepare for their future and gives them added advantage in this ever-competitive world.

Thus, setting up an abacus education centre is an excellent great proposition with low investment, low risk, great opportunity and above all, a mode for self-satisfaction and sense of achievement.